Tao te CHING

THE Tao te CHING

A Zen Poet's View

WRITTEN AND ILLUSTRATED BY D. R. STREETER

Gibbs Smith, Publisher
Salt Lake City

First Edition
10 09 08 07 06   5 4 3 2 1

Published by
Gibbs Smith, Publisher
P.O. Box 667
Layton, Utah 84041

Orders: 1.800.748.5439
www.gibbs-smith.com

Design by Catherine Lau Hunt
Printed and bound in Canada

Library of Congress Cataloging-in-Publication Data

Streeter, D. R.
    The Tao te ching : a Zen poet's view / written and illustrated by
    D. R. Streeter. — 1st ed.
      p. cm.
    ISBN 1-4236-0003-7
    1. Laozi. Dao de jing.   I. Title.
    BL1900.L35S77 2006
    299.5′1482 — dc22

2005033873

Poetry is a precise vehicle

for those who know how to use

its emptiness

Introduction

The Tao [Dao]
1. Knowledge that exists beyond our consciousness.
2. A dark knowledge, much like the face of the new moon, hidden yet full of mystery.
3. A way to know without knowing.

The *Tao Te Ching* (sometimes translated as "the path ahead" or simply "The Way") is an ancient text consisting of eighty-one chapters or sayings ascribed to Lao Tzu (600 BC), a keeper of the archives and sacred books at the imperial court in ancient China.

Some time ago I was in the midst of a rather deep and philosophical conversation with an old and very wise monk. He was a man who measured his words and seldom wasted time coming to the point; someone who had dedicated his life to the fine art of contemplation. As we spoke about mystical theology and the contemplative life, I began to realize that the conversation kept swinging back to the here and now.

I remember asking him what scriptures and texts he was reading at the time. He replied, "I'm not." He then reached into the folds of his long gray robe and pulled out a tattered copy of a poem written by a twelfth-century contemplative and mystic. It seems to me that only mystics can speak of mysticism and they must do so in poetic form. Poetry is indeed the language of the contemplative life.

As we approach the profound wisdom of the *Tao Te Ching*, we need to remember that the author was a poet and that much of the wisdom and instruction is hidden in plain sight. Poets have a rather clever way of doing that. To look at the words and phrases directly may not be the best way to approach them. Perhaps it would be better to come to the *Tao Te Ching* as you would come to an empty rice field illuminated by a new moon. A poet is more interested in reflected light than in intense bright light. Better to have the eyes relaxed and slightly closed than to have them opened wide attempting to *see something.*

But why, then, should we try to explain the mystery of the *Tao Te Ching* anyway? Explaining is something that the poet avoids at all costs. If you wish the scripture-like text to reveal itself, it is better to blend with the words or characters. Better yet to let the words or characters go by and view them from the other side, like watching the dark side of the moon float through the empty sky.

If words could ever have a three-dimensional quality, these would surely be the ones. Poetry is like that. Works of art that are considered "masterpieces" have that kind of depth. They cannot be exhausted by looking at them, listening to them or reading them. Such is the way of the Tao. If we let the teachings of the *Tao Te Ching* "sink in," let them quietly rest within by being contemplative about them, the wisdom of the *Tao Te Ching* will rise to the surface like cream rises to the top of milk.

I have often thought about just how Lao Tzu wrote the *Tao Te Ching.* When Lao Tzu, as legend has it, handed over his work to the border guard of Hanku Pass in order to be allowed to proceed, did he just give him a copy?

Did he give him the original (as a true renunciant would probably do)? Or perhaps he just hung out with the guard and wrote it then and there. (Historians say the characters were painted on bamboo sticks.) Could it have been that simple? We might consider that some of the most sublime music ever created was written as fast as the composer could put it down. Mozart is a good example.

The words of Lao Tzu make us feel good. They also make a lot of sense. They answer, and will continue to answer, questions that come from living in a world that is determined to destroy itself. Scripture is like that. Poetry is like that. Great works of art and the *Tao Te Ching* are like that.

Even if the world succeeds in its self-destruction, the Tao, or the "Great Way" will continue on, waiting for another unique and wonderfully wise character like old Lao to come strolling down the road on his way to a hermitage somewhere in the mountain wilderness.

Although I follow the contours of many translations of the *Tao Te Ching*, the phrasing is original. I used as a reference source *Lao-Tzu's Taoteching*, an excellent translation by Red Pine. His precise account along with commentaries gave me a clear framework from which to work.

—D. R. Streeter

Words of wisdom
are so simple
Just look for them
in ordinary things

❧

Then you will go beyond
their face value
To the mysteries they contain

❧

THE

TAO

Tao

From the south

warm wind

Clouds spill over

A million pounds of water

fall down

A million more float through the sky

Who can say

that something

does not come from nothing

The one who works the land

speaks simple words

that reduce what is complex

He says, "Harvest the fields in the fall

Cultivate in the spring

Irrigate in the heat of summer"

His words are easy to understand

yet require much effort to fulfill

The ancient ones used similar words

to tell us of the Tao

They say, "Just let things be in their own way

Do not cherish opinions

Hold fast to the Great Image

Abandon strategies"

These words also require much effort

to fulfill

The ancient ones spoke of the Great Way

in the same manner the farmer speaks of a road

that cuts through a field of grain

One speaks of the way of heaven

the other speaks of the way of the earth

Neither is above the other

Therefore the sage keeps the jewel of wisdom

beneath simple clothes

bright

If the sun moves too close

the sea will boil over

and every living creature

will die

Therefore

illumination is keeping

the right distance

The immense power

of heaven and earth

cannot extend a life

beyond its limits

The way means "just this"

There is nothing more

Success is success

Failure is failure

Nothing mysterious

Nothing hidden

This alone

is the Great Teaching

To make use of the Tao

is like taking a cup of sea water

from the ocean

One cup removed

does not diminish the whole

A cup of sea water

can be controlled with no effort

The ocean itself is influenced only

by the moon

Such large things

are beyond the human person

It is better to let them be

Just examine closely the small amount

Do so with focus and determination

In this way you will grasp

what cannot be seen

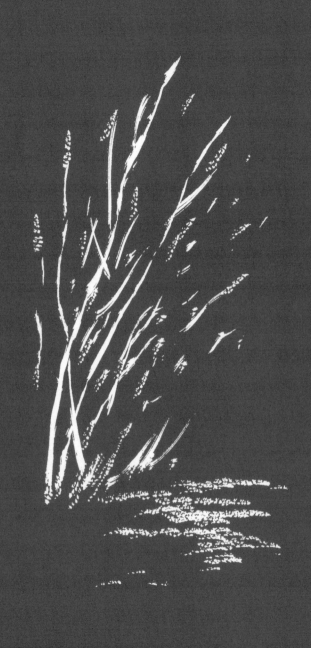

There are some things

that feed the soul of man

Things that are incredible

Indescribable

and

without impurity

But they are the kinds of things that vanish

with too much learning

Yin and Yang work together

to produce harmony

Harmony is the root of existence

and nonexistence

The wall between existence

and nonexistence

is like a thick glass wall

With great effort it can be shattered

and stepped through

Existence and nonexistence

are separate and yet they are not separate

This saying must be pondered

day and night

If you seek definition

you will lose the whole

If one word is misplaced

heaven and earth collapse

What is already perfect

does not need repair

Life from beginning to end

can be seen in one glance

Mountains, rivers and lakes

the stars and sky

can also be seen

The eye on the left

can see the female principle

The eye on the right

can see the male principle

The eye of the interior

can see the still point

at the center

Therefore

things give birth to things

by uniting the male and the female

The Tao is not united

Even so

its wholeness is complete

When a mother gives birth

something soft and supple

comes into the world

When the soft and supple

become hard and stiff

what was given is taken away

When a leaf is soft and tender

it can break through hard clay

When it is hard and stiff

it doesn't move at all

What is rigid

is dead

This includes the body and mind

It is said

What is soft and supple

will bend without breaking

To rule the world

means to guard the gate

The people feel safe

The high official seems like an attendant

Sovereign power

appears no different

than a handshake

When the people are not aware

that they are being ruled

they share the kingdom's wealth

In the vast horizon

clouds form

Ten thousand images

are plainly in view

Towering mountains

dark forests

and deep valleys

change color and shape

with each ray of sunlight

with each gust of wind

There is abundance

but the people cannot see it

Unnatural

replaces natural

The Great Way appears

then disappears

When the Tao becomes visible

it never stays the same

The moon is full and becomes half full

So it is with the Tao

Inside the seed

there is an image

Inside a creature

there is an image

Look silently within

There too you find an image

If the teacher needs inspiration

to teach

his work is not authentic

Who can benefit

Why should the student

praise the teacher

Why should the teacher

praise the student

It serves no purpose

Both become distracted

To learn what is real

be real

The sublime is found

in plain knowing

Its light is concealed

Both teacher and student

benefit from it

No one is left behind

This is called "going blind

and seeing"

Going deaf

and hearing

Growing numb and feeling

Appearing simple

remaining profound

Across the way

the carpenter's hammer

strikes the nail like a Zen bell

Even here

emptiness can be found

A great leader

extends his hand

to his opposition

He remains close

to the center of activity

Without stretching his bow

he wins the battle

His gait is like a tiger

His strides are soft

like a small child

His steps cannot be confined

to long or short

His feet penetrate the surface

of the earth

He rules his own life

in the same way he rules

ten thousand chariots

In the thin line

of fragile green

just above hard rocks

and clay

just beside the mountains

and the shore

in between the stars at night

between the sun and shade

the Tao is just

a winding path

nothing more

Let the mind be open

Let the mouth remain shut

Things arise from things

Mountains become deserts

Deserts become mountains

Clouds become rain

Lakes become oceans

Each cycle is completed

from the greatest

to the smallest

Hence there is no profit in learning

The Great Way has a mind of its own

To pursue knowledge

is like being a wheel that continues to turn

even though the cart stopped

long ago

Those who are considered "Great"
are like a cell
The cell has six sides
The floor represents humility
Two of the walls
Yin and Yang
The window represents vision
The door a gateway
The ceiling
knowledge

Therefore the sage is completely evolved
but does not boast
Seems perfectly balanced
but does not "stand out"
Possesses great insight
and is considered wise
Moves freely from "within"
to "without"

On the roadside

an old monk

All his possessions

are contained

within

The people travel

from here to there

coming

going

Their destination

reverses itself

over and over again

The Tao remains firmly

planted in one place

and yet cannot be left behind

Four kings guard

East, West, North, and South

The paths they guard

are precious

and cannot be separated

Each has a color

that can't be blended

Each has a sound

that can't be imitated

The center remains still

It has no color or sound

yet the rest could not exist

without it

Plants catch the mist

Storms pass by

Thunder comes from thin air

Torrential rains come

from floating clouds

A pine cone falls

A bird cries

Reality without poetry

is like squaring

something round

To appear to be without honor

To appear to be without wealth

To appear to be without power

It's like being a tree too twisted

and crooked to be cut down

The sage hides his inner wealth

He seems like a beggar

He covers his immense power

and seems harmless enough

He distracts the learned ones

He relies on wisdom rather than words

When healing comes he will say

"It came by itself"

When he defeats his enemies he claims

"It was just luck"

Without pride there is no envy

Humility is his choice of weapons

He lives his life

without interruption

He has learned his art through

suffering and resolve

He ministers to others

and at the center of transformation

he has found a peaceful place

Outside

beneath the windowpane

a dazed blackbird

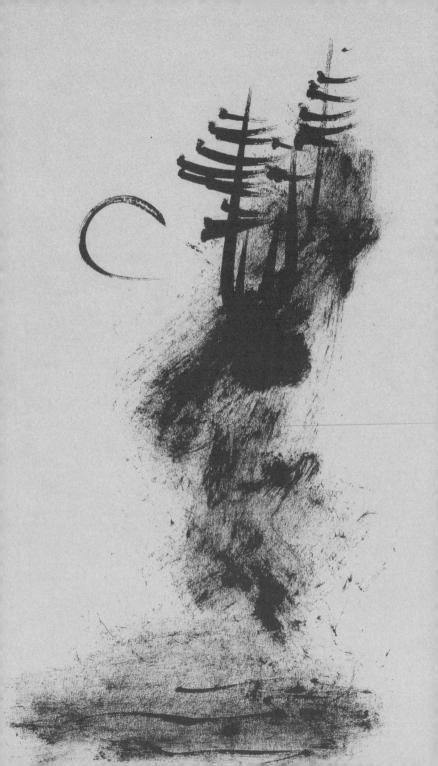

Great teachers
do not rely on books
There is no guide
to emptiness
The opening must be found
through endurance
Patience is the virtue
that unearths heaven's gate

Only through excavation
is the ancient city revealed
To find the king
means to find the Great Way

The king lives outside of boundaries
His words will never be known
or understood
Scholars will interpret
Mystics will be elated
The common people
will laugh out loud

On the tree

branches form

brilliant green

Who decides when

or how

The people of the village

sit close together

They seem happy and glad

They mingle as they gather in the village square

Off in the castles and mansions

the people are separate and confined

behind tall walls

Their smiles seem shallow

and no one tells the truth

Those who have little

seem filled with abundance

They have compassion and care for others

Their friendships

are as valuable as pure gold

Those who have great treasures

seem important and secure

They are surrounded by luxury and wear fine clothes

but they live in fear of losing

and have no time for others

Eat without tasting

Seek comfort from what cannot give life

One is full and happy

The other is empty and sad

Therefore it is best to examine closely

the meaning of wealth

Distant mountains

brilliant green

Within the house

a room of dreams

The Tao is called
The Great Way
Why is the Tao called The Great Way
Because no matter where you touch it
what is alive comes out
In the way of the Tao
all things combined
work perfectly together
Yin becomes Yang
Yang becomes Yin
The female joins the male
The male joins the female
One gives to the other

No matter how much is needed
by one or the other
the Tao does not hold back
With no effort it gives exactly
the right amount

Wise men reach out for wisdom
Musicians reach out for song
Poets reach out for words
The sage does not reach out
at all

The big black crow

gathers twigs

from the branch

Its huge long beak

breaks them off

with ease

When water is warm and flowing

there is nothing more comfortable

to be in

As it cools down and becomes ice

it will be avoided at all costs

The Tao is like a meandering stream

on a warm summer day

Therefore

the Tao is inviting

If it were not inviting

it would not be the Tao

If learning is forced

it will soon be forgotten

The Tao is not so mysterious

when the stomach is empty

To follow the Great Way means

to find something to eat

Water seems weak as it passes

over the shallow rocks and rapids

It gathers strength

as it accumulates and enters deep channels

It becomes destructive with the winter rains

It moves a million tons of earth

with great ease

It takes from one place and gives to another

It floods the farmland to bring nutrition

It provides fish for the people to eat

and transports their goods

It becomes calm and deep

like a jade pool

It is the primary teacher

of the Great Way

In the midst of battle
The warrior is the center of calm
his sword flashing, cutting and then
disappearing into thin air
In one moment
his body is hard like stone
In the next
soft like water
In his mind
bright light
and an eye that can see
in all directions
He doesn't think
before he moves
His life depends on it

Because his mind is pure
and bright
he sees others as he sees himself
He honors his enemy
He knows that his life
won or lost
is the same as theirs

Our ancestors performed

a great service

by dying

If there were no death

life would be impossible

If there were no chance

there would be nothing to risk

If heaven consisted of eternal praise

boredom would surely come

If our ancestors had no descendants

there would be none to work the fields

and sing the harvest songs

The lesson here is this

"Let go and let the Tao unfold"

True meditation

is written on one blade of grass

It unfolds like a scroll

Two wise men hold it open

Their coarse gray robes

brush the ground

Their eyes are radiant

They haven't spoken for a thousand years

They haven't made a sound

Off in the distance

a wild bird flies south

Beneath tall cliffs

nests are empty

The sage lives beneath others

like the vagrant beneath the bridge

Gold chariots pass by

yet he is content with what he has

His teaching is simple

and without words

His life goes by unnoticed

He succeeds without effort

and so he finds his place

where there once was none

There are very few who can equal this

Near the stream

dew gathers

A frog leaps

on slippery stones

The warrior wears thick armor

to protect himself

He eats his food for strength not taste

He stays aware and in good health

For him staying in good health

means to stay alive

His training is endless

Night and day he must choose

the best strategies for his life

For him each moment is priceless

and must be savored like fine wine

His life has no weak spots

for the opposition to attack

The warrior survives battle

after battle and uses death

as his adviser

The common person lives as

if there were no death

He takes his vitality for granted

He wastes his life force for material gain

and comfort

His inheritance consists of

a small portion of earth

His life was lived

somewhere else

When things are not enough

there is striving

When shape does not conform to shape

there is frustration

To increase or decrease

what is given

creates something artificial

What is artificial does not last

The sage achieves perfection

without changing a thing

His wisdom is simple

and cannot be embellished

with this or that

The sound of laughing

drifts through the house of concubines

In the morning the lesson is clear

Nothing lasts forever

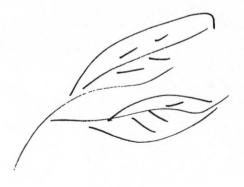

Open the gate of heaven

You will find the female

powerful

bright

and yet unseen

Inhale the moon

Exhale the sun

You will rule the world

and all its treasures

Keep things in their place

The sun above

The moon below

Store the essence

and you will understand

Dark Virtue

Great talkers collect knowledge
for the sake of talking
They make their living
with their tongue
They seem thoughtful and are poised
in public
Not so thoughtful or poised
when no one is around

Those who speak what's true
may not be noticed
Their words
are few
They help others
before they help themselves
They live without struggling
They act without contending

They know
there is not one thing
that is not revealed
This is the nature
of the Tao

Without competition

there is no award

Who cares who's keeping score

If there were nothing to buy

gold would have no value

No prizes to take home

Nothing to steal

Just follow the rule of wisdom

Emptiness, emptiness beyond the mind

Nourish the inside

Soften the outside

Strengthen the center

The guard remains awake

His sword is never dull

Too close to be seen

Too distant to be a threat

The swift hawk

seems to fall from the sky

Twisting, turning, disappearing

in its prey

The world is divided

into five parts

There are five seasons

winter, spring, summer, late summer

and fall

There are five colors

red, yellow, blue, green

and white

There are five sacred sounds

and five pairs of internal organs

The Rule of Wisdom says this

"Use just enough

and leave the rest"

The Jewel of Knowledge says this

"Better to be guided from within

than from without"

With no line of distinction

there is freedom

Having is the same

as not having

Hard is no different from soft

Without trying to be good

there is good

Without trying to be kind

there is kindness

Instinct becomes life force

With one lesson

there is perfection

With no effort

comes the flawless shape

All things are completed

There is nothing

not achieved

On the front of the owl's chest

strange designs

The sound it makes

is impossible to trace

The Way is like a circle

Heaven and earth inside

Eternal, immortal

just names

Nothing kept, no possessions

Given a place in the rear

ending up in front

Not guarded

not harmed

Whatever is sought

can be found

This is the natural Way

emptiness

Light precedes
the rising sun—we call it dawn
Light lingers on after sunset—
we call it dusk
Knowledge precedes birth—
we call that instinct
After death we call it rebirth

Those who speak the truth
know this
Therefore they help others
by being self-renewed
They do not race toward time
They refuse to compete
When hunger comes
they eat
When fatigue comes
they sleep
Their vision originates from within
Each day given to them
is received as a great gift
They gain wisdom
by walking along the path

Clear water reveals

Thick bark protects

The eye is small

but can see mountains

The ears can hear the buzz

of insects

Where is the line

that separates

the Tao from man

Along the Path   .

The Ten Thousand Things

say "there is none"

Counting all the wars
that were ever fought
who can remember the victor
Like a room without a door
death serves no purpose

There is one who defeats
and there is one
who is defeated
The one who knows that
neither wins
is superior

Sadness in the kingdom
comes from mourning the dead
What was so alive
is now silent
The great hero
honored far and wide
would still much rather
be alive

The fields are empty

The grain mill is silent

An old yellow cat

stalks a mouse

The tree is equal to
the creatures that live
in and around it
How is this so
Being equal means
"no gain, no loss"
When leaves fall to the ground
the ground is nourished
and enriched
It becomes dark and soft and warm
Being soft and warm
it is inviting to many tiny creatures
The soil beneath becomes alive
with activity
The activity attracts other forms of life
Birds build their nests
Owls sleep there at night
Many of the bugs and insects are
consumed and digested
In this way their little bodies
nourish the tree

The bugs depend on
the tree
The tree depends on the bugs
This is what is meant by
"no gain, no loss"

It is emptiness

that makes the vessel useful

Fired clay has a dull finish

Rice grain is kept inside

The Tao is never empty

yet is never filled

Better to be nourished

from within

than from without

Consider the pail of rain

It is filled to the brim

and yet the opening is small

Although the mountains are vast

and steep

they are covered with snow

Block out what is lost

Seek what is real

Delusions abound

Find the Tao

wherever you look

Listen to the whispers

beneath the artificial sounds

There is no place

the Great Way

is not revealed

What is born, dies

What dies is reborn

The old tree

just inside the gate

still flowers in the spring

Soft pink blossoms

still cover the ground

Although emptiness

is vast and deep

only a small portion

can be used

It's like drawing water

from a spring

Ten thousand generations

mother, father, child

mother, father, child

from the beginning

to the end

This is a great mystery

yet is considered natural

I really can't say what it is

I am left without words

There is nothing to lose or gain

Life will go on

I can afford to be generous

I have nothing to fear or hate

No one to distrust or envy

The Way means to keep all this

in mind

In the old pond

a lone white duck

has joined a flock

of gray and black

coots

The white duck

and the rather large group

of black and gray mud coots

waddle about and peck at the wet ground from

morning 'til night

The white duck has learned

to do all the things that mud coots do

The coots are not the least bit

offended

Even though this seems to go

against the nature of things

and seems a little odd

there is no code

or rule that has been broken

There is no discrimination

There is no retaliation

Therefore

it is best to be color-blind

to see the truth of color

It is best to be led around

as though blind to see others

in the right light

And in order to live in perfect harmony

it is best to paddle around aimlessly

without trying to "do something"

or be "somebody"

Try to think about it

and the Tao becomes wooden

Like a dead tree

it loses its origin

To think about it

is to extend

what is here and now

The circle extends to the tips of the fingers

There is nothing more

The Great Way is the lungs breathing

the heart beating

and the limbs moving

like a living tree

Therefore

the Tao is content

with small things

Small things reflect great things

There is no need to pursue it

anymore

I alone have no parents

I have no words to speak

There is nothing I wish to hear

or see

I have no knowledge

I can call my own

I have nothing to give

or keep

I do know when enough is enough

and I do know there are few

that are truly free